Take A Wetlands

By Jane Kirkland
Edited by
Rob Kirkland
Dorothy Burke
Melanie Palaisa

Are You Ready to Discover...

I have had many wetlands adventures. But one of my favorites happened right in my own neighborhood. One June morning at 7 a.m. my phone rang. It was my neighbor Carol. "Come quickly!" she whispered. "There's a monster in my yard. And bring your field guide".

"Cool!" I said. "A monster!" I grabbed some field guides and my camera on the way out the door. Of course, I didn't bother to look for my field guide to monsters—there is no such thing! So I brought my bird, reptile, and mammal guides with me. When I got to Carol's house, she was standing in her front yard and another neighbor, Jacki, was standing in Carol's flower bed. Jacki had a broom and she was brushing off the shell of a really huge turtle. The turtle had dug a hole with its hind legs and the back half of its body was down in the hole. The turtle was covered with dirt and I guess Jacki thought she was helping it by brushing off the dirt.

"Can you identify this turtle?" Jacki said. "It's the biggest turtle I've ever seen!"

I didn't know anything about turtles. I paged through my field guide and quickly discovered that there sure are a lot of different species of turtles. Finally, I found a turtle in the book that looked just like the one in the garden. It was huge—and not very attractive. "Jacki," I called out. "Does that turtle look like it has a dinosaur tail?" Jacki answered, "Sure does."

Quickly I stood up and yelled out, "Jacki, step away from the turtle—it's a *Snapping* Turtle! She is here to lay her eggs. And she can hurt us if she feels threatened!" Jacki stepped away and we all watched the turtle from a safe distance. When she was done laying her eggs, she returned to the lake. It was a very cool discovery and I'll never forget my first-ever Snapping Turtle sighting.

A Day to Remember

I hope you have exciting adventures on your wetlands walk. I hope you discover birds, plants, insects, mammals, crabs and more! And if you should come across a Snapping Turtle, please stay away from it!

I'm so happy that I took my camera to Carol's house that day. This turtle laid about thirty eggs! Snapping Turtles can be found in the eastern half of North America.

...Nature in a Wetland?

The lake where I live is a wetland. Snapping Turtles are only one of the species of turtles that live here. There are also other reptiles and amphibians, wildflowers, insects, spiders, butterflies, moths, trees, birds, mammals, and more!

This book will help you prepare for your wetland walk so you can find exciting plants and animals, too. It is divided into three sections: *Get Ready, Get Set,* and *Go.* You can read this book in any order you wish. Here in the *Get Ready* section I'll explain what a wetland is and show you several kinds of wetlands.

Wetlands are great places to see Bald Eagles. Their habitat is lakes, streams, marshes, and seacoasts with large bodies of water and tall trees where they can nest. I hope you see a Bald Eagle on one of your wetland walks.

In the *Get Set* section you'll learn about some very special wetland residents and about the unique features that help them to survive and thrive in wetlands.

The *Go* section will teach you which plants and animals to look for in the different wetlands. It also contains a page for you to take field notes, a page to record your observations, and photos to help you identify the plants and animals you find.

Throughout this book you'll find artwork and essays by kids, you'll read about other wetland adventures, and you'll read fun and interesting sidebars.

Once you know where to look and what to look for you'll see just how exciting wetlands can be! You'll wonder why you never thought of a wetland as a nursery or food factory. You'll understand that wetlands are not only cool places to explore, they are very important habitats. Then you'll start to notice wildlife and plants you never noticed before and you'll wonder, "How did I not see these things before today?" Soon, you'll have your own wetlands adventures to talk about. Are you ready to discover nature at the wetlands?

Be Prepared

Go safely: Stay on trails and boardwalks. Don't go alone—that's never a good idea.

Take nothing away: Never take plants or animals from the wetlands.

Leave nothing behind: Don't leave food, trash, or anything else behind.

Get Ready! What Makes a...

New Words?

Habitat (HAB-i-tat):

Where something lives. A plant or animal's habitat is the part of the environment in which it lives.

Recognize These?

The pond illustrated here is a wetland. You can see some of the common animals found in freshwater wetlands.

Can you find the Red-winged Blackbird, Mallard ducks, Monarch butterfly, Common Green Darner dragonfly, and Bullfrog? Can you think of any other animals you might find in and around a pond?

Keywords and Phrases

To learn more search for "what is a wetland" on the Web.

To explore a wetland, you first have to find one. To find one, you have to know what to look for. There are many different types of wetlands but, in general, three factors make a wetland a wetland. They are:

Hydrophytic vegetation. (hy-dro-FIT-ic). A wetland must be home to plants that can live in wet soil—hydrophytic plants. These plants are called **hydrophytes** (HY-dro-fites).

Hydric Soils. Soil that has poor drainage and is so saturated with water that it has little or no oxygen is called hydric soil.

Wetland Hydrology. The land must be covered by water or the soil soaked with water long enough during the year (not necessarily all year long, though) to cause the soil to be hydric and to allow hydrophytes to thrive.

A wetland is an ecosystem: a place where plants and animals interact with one another. Within that ecosystem, there might be several kinds of **habitats**. Wetlands are found throughout the world.

...Wetland a Wetland?

The water in a wetland can be *lotic* (running water) such as the water in a river, stream, or creek. The water can be *lentic* (standing water) such as a lake, pond, or marsh. Wetlands are diverse—there are many kinds of wetlands and many **species** of plants and animals that live in different wetlands.

Depending on where you live, there might be one or several kinds of wetlands nearby. I selected a variety of wetlands to include in this book, so you will hopefully find at least one kind near you.

Take this book with you when you travel. You can explore different wetlands wherever you go. The more you explore, the more you'll discover!

A cattail is not a cat's tail but a plant that grows in wetlands. Can you find the cattails in the pond scene below? There are five silly cartoons in this book. My nephew Christian drew the cartoons. I wrote the silly captions and poems.

New Word?

Species (SPEE-shees)
A certain kind, variety, or type of living creature.

Know Where You Can Go

Wetlands are fragile habitats. Be careful not to harm any plants or animals. Stay on paths, boardwalks, or trails.

Where are the Mosquitoes?

This book doesn't celebrate mosquitoes, rats, ticks, and other pests that live in wetlands. It's not that these animals aren't important. But they are pests and there are only 32 pages in this book. I'd much rather use the space to talk about the exciting and cool plants and animals of the wetlands.

Get Ready to Become a...

Scientifically Speaking

Wetlands can be divided into two major systems: saltwater and freshwater. Within those, there are five major categories of wetlands. They are::

Marine (muh-REEN): coastal, saltwater wetlands. Marine means "of the sea".

Estuarine (ESS-choo-uh-reen): coastal wetlands where river water meets ocean water, creating a mixture of fresh and salt water. Estuarine means "of an estuary".

Lacustrine (luh-KUS-treen): inland freshwater wetlands around lakes and reservoirs. Lacustrine means "of a lake".

Palustrine (puh-LUS-treen): isolated, inland freshwater wetlands that are not a part of a lake or reservoir. Palustrine means "of a marsh".

Riverine (RIV-uh-reen): freshwater wetlands along moving waters such as rivers and streams. Usually (but not always) inland wetlands. Riverine means "of a river".

Coastal Vs. Inland

Coastal wetlands are found in coastal watersheds. These are watersheds that drain into the ocean, an estuary, or a bay. All other wetlands are inland wetlands.

Clean water is vital to our planet. What we put in our water such as industrial waste, affects the quality of the water in our watershed. What we put on the ground that seeps into the water such as chemicals and fertilizers on our lawns and farmland, affects the quality of the water in our watershed. What we pour down the drain affects the quality of the water in our watershed. So much of what we do affects our watersheds.

But wait. Do you even know what a watershed is? A watershed is a drainage basin.

Water doesn't stand still. It flows downhill. A watershed is the area of land that water flows over, under, and through on its way to a larger drainage basin, such as a large river or an ocean. A watershed not only includes the land and the water, it includes the plants, animals, and humans that live there. The wetlands you explore are part of some watershed. The creeks, rivers, and lakes that you boat, fish, or swim in are part of a watershed.

Which wetland would you prefer; the one in the top photo or the one on the bottom? The health of our wetlands depends on the health of our watersheds. How's your watershed doing?

The health of the water you swim or bathe in, drink, and do your laundry in depends on the health of your watershed.

To learn more about your watershed ask your teacher or do some research at your library or on the Web. To find out the name and website of your watershed, visit: **epa.gov/surf.**

...Wetland and Watershed Wizard

I live near a wetland and I love exploring it. Wetlands are important to our planet. I hope this book will help people (like you) to appreciate wetlands, too. So before you head out to explore, I'd like to share some of the ways that wetlands help us:

Wetlands are important habitats. They are habitats for many plants and animals. Some animals live in wetlands all their lives. Others spend part of their lives there.

Wetlands are buffer zones. Wetlands help to protect us from floods by acting like sponges. They soak up water that might otherwise flood our homes, roads, and land.

Wetlands are breeding grounds. Fish, birds, amphibians, shellfish, and other animals breed in wetlands.

Wetlands provide food. Plants, insects, bacteria, amphibians, fungi and more that are found in wetlands are part of the food chain. And we even grow important food for humans in wetlands such as rice and cranberries.

Wetlands help to clean our water. The plants and soils in wetlands help to purify water before it becomes groundwater and drinking water. Wetland plants can even help to remove chemicals, pesticides and metal from water.

My husband Rob and I like to explore the wetland where we live. We sometimes canoe around the lake with Lou, our neighbor's dog (and my favorite bulldog). We always take our camera to take photos of things like these beautiful water lilies.

Common Names for Wetlands

Most people know wetlands by their common names such as swamps, marshes, prairie potholes, lakes, ponds, floodplains, cypress swamps, rivers, and streams. WOW. Are there really that many types of wetlands? Yes—and even more!

Do the Math

Scientists estimate that every 2.7 miles of healthy wetlands can reduce a storm surge (vertically) by one foot. The surge from hurricane Katrina in 2005 was anywhere from 22-28 feet. How many miles of healthy wetlands were needed to protect New Orleans?

Who Cares? They Do!

The **Chesapeake Bay Foundation (CBF)** is the largest conservation organization dedicated solely to saving the Chesapeake Bay watershed—which is huge! Their motto is "Save the Bay". Learn more at:

www. cbf.org

Wetland scene by Zoe Thompson, age 12, of Tahoe City, CA.

New Words

Vertebrate
(VER-te-brate)

Animals that have backbones, or spines. Their skeletons are internal. You are a vertebrate. So are monkeys, snakes, frogs, birds, and fish. Invertebrates are animals without backbones, like jellyfish, earthworms, and insects.

Frog or Toad

How are frogs and toads different from each other?

Frogs live mostly in or near water. Their skin is smooth and thin. Toads live mostly on dry land. Their skin is rough and warty.

Most species of frogs taste good to predators. So they are built for quick escapes: bulging eyes help them to see well, skinny bodies and long legs help them to hop long distances. Webbed feet help them to swim fast.

Toads have poison glands behind their eyes which make them taste bad to predators. Predators pretty much leave them alone. So toads don't need to hop far; they can walk instead.

Frogs lay their eggs in clusters. Toads lay their eggs in long chains.

Keywords and Phrases

To learn more search for "indicator species" and "Life cycle of a frog" on the Web.

Wetlands are home to lots of *amphibians* (am-FIB-e-ans). Amphibians are **vertebrates** that start life as aquatic larvae with gills. Then they develop lungs which they use to breathe air when they are adults. Frogs and salamanders are amphibians.

Frogs might be the most popular of all the amphibians. After all, they don't bite, they are cute (in a strange sort of way), and they make great sounds. Bullfrogs are my favorite frogs—do you have a favorite?

There are several stages to a frog's life: egg, tadpole, froglet, and frog. With a little luck maybe you can find frogs in all stages of their life when you visit a wetland.

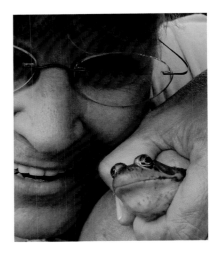

Frogs are "bioindicators", an indication of the quality of the wetland. In other words, if frogs are present and healthy, that means the wetland is healthy.

Look for frog eggs and tadpoles in shallow water. Depending on the species, tadpoles can hatch from eggs in just a few days.

The change that takes place from tadpole to frog is called metamorphosis (met-ah-MORE-feh-sis), which means "to change in form". The amount of time it takes to change from a tadpole to a frog depends on the species. For Wood frogs, it can take 20 days to change from an egg to a tadpole and 2 months to change from a tadpole to a frog.

Each frog egg is inside a jelly-like casing to protect it.

H ow long a tadpole stays a tadpole depends on the species of frog. In Bullfrogs, tadpoles can stay tadpoles for up to 3 years! Tadpoles breathe through gills but grow lungs during their lifespan, which they will use when they become frogs. Tadpoles have long tails. They live in the water. The tadpole will grow a pair of back legs first, then it will grow front legs. When it has legs some people call it a "tadpole with legs" and others call it a "froglet". The froglet's tail gets smaller until it disappears and the froglet becomes a frog.

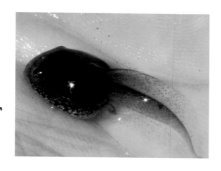

The longer a tadpole stays a tadpole, the larger it will be when it becomes a frog.

Frogs breathe through their lungs but continue to hang out in water. That's because oxygen can pass from the water through the frog's skin into the frog's blood. For this to happen, their skin must remain moist at all times.

A froglet is a tadpole with legs. It absorbs its tail and uses the energy to nourish itself. Yum—not!

Bullfrogs can live as long as 9 years! Exactly how long they live probably depends on how many birds and other frog-eating predators they have to dodge in their lifetime.

When people think of metamorphosis, they think of butterflies—not frogs. Oh well, it isn't easy being green!

See the circle behind the Bullfrog's eye? That's the ear circle. If the circle is much bigger than the eye, the frog is a male. If it is the same size or smaller, the Bullfrog is a female.

Become a Citizen Scientist

Frogwatch USA is a citizen science program. Citizen scientists are people who study science as a hobby and report their findings to a group of scientists to help them gather information about plants and animals. I wish that at least one member of every family in North America (or the world for that matter) were a citizen scientist.

You can become a citizen scientist, learn about and help frogs and toads by joining Frogwatch USA. Learn more at:

www.nwf.org/frogwatchUSA

Corner Frogs?

Yes, the three frogs in the photo on the headers of this book are Bullfrogs.

Keywords and Phrases:

To learn more, search for "indicator species" and "Life cycle of a frog" on the Web.

Ole! Now this is my idea of a bullfrog!

Get Set to Study My Cuddly...

Got Field Guides?

We live in a big country. There are many kinds of wetlands and many species of plants and animals that inhabit those wetlands. There's a good chance that you'll see plants or animals in your wetland that you don't see in this book. And you'll probably see some in this book that you won't see in your wetlands.

At some point, you might want a field guide or two to help you identify more plants and animals. There are many styles and sizes of field guides that cover many topics. How do you decide which is best for you? Visit the nature section of the library or bookstore with an adult and look at the various kinds of guides. Choose the one that you like best. It's that simple and it's that personal. ☺

Keywords and phrases

To learn more, search for "turtle", terrapin", and "tortoise" on the Web.

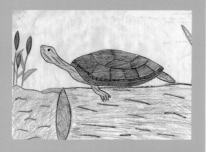

Turtle by Morgan Stefanacci, age 11, of Merchantville, NJ.

Another very popular animal of wetlands is the turtle. There are lots of species of turtles that live in wetlands but perhaps the most well-known is the Painted Turtle. It is so well known because it is the most widespread turtle in North America. It's also one of the easiest to see because Painted Turtles love to bask in the sun and sometimes you can see a large group of them crowded on a single log!

Painted Turtles are reptiles. They breathe air. They are cold-blooded, meaning their body temperature rises and falls with the temperature of their environment. They live in the water but lay eggs on land. They can lay 1 to 2 clutches (groups of eggs) a year. Each clutch can have from 2 to 20 eggs. Sometimes hatchlings (newly-hatched turtles) spend their first winter in the nest and don't come out at all until spring.

The carapace (KARE-uh-pace) is the topside of a turtle's shell. The plastron is the underside. Of the four painted turtles, Eastern, Midland, Southern and Western, the Western (below) has the prettiest plastron. The carapaces of Painted Turtles look similar except the Southern, which has a red line down the middle.

Painted turtles live in shallow streams, rivers with slow moving water, or lakes and ponds. They live in my lake and are one of my favorite animals to photograph. I can sneak up quietly in my canoe while they bask on logs. Young painted turtles are carnivores (meat eaters), but as they get older they add plants to their diet which makes them omnivores.

Turtles are struggling to survive in a world where their habitat is disappearing. Turtles get run over by cars and kidnapped by kids who take them home to keep as pets. Wild turtles should stay wild, don't you think? Who wants to live in a fish bowl, anyway?

...Mud-puddly Painted Buddy

One morning several years ago I saw a Painted Turtle in the meadow behind my house. I knew she had laid eggs, otherwise she wouldn't have been in the meadow. I found her nest—it wasn't difficult because the dirt was freshly piled on top of the nest. I didn't dare disturb it. It's my understanding that nest temperature plays an important part in reptile nests. That night I made a little sign on a post so I could put it near the nest and count the days until the hatchlings would emerge. I wanted to be there when it happened! But the next day, when I returned to the nest with my sign, the ground was torn up. I could see raccoon tracks nearby. I guess a raccoon found the nest during the night.

Painted Turtles share their basking spaces with other turtles (above), snakes (right) and even alligators (below). If you look closely at the alligator picture you'll also see a softshell turtle to the left of the alligator. He looks as if he's going to climb up onto the alligator!

Turtle Predators

Even though turtles have strong shells to protect them, they still have predators. Raccoons, snakes, skunks, foxes, and even crows will raid their nests. Young turtles are eaten by raccoons as well as herons, bullfrogs, fish and even snapping turtles. Adult turtles are eaten by raccoons, osprey, and even Bald Eagles.

Free Coloring Book

Get a free wetlands coloring book by downloading the PDF file at:

www. fws.gov/nwi/educator.htm

Free Cloud Book

Precipitation plays a key role in wetlands. Learn about weather by downloading a free copy of Take a Cloud Walk at:

www. takeawalk.com

Wren by Sarah Applegate, age 12, of Moorestown, NJ.

11

Go! Take Some Fields Notes

Your Field Notes Page

Use this form or blank paper for your field notes. If you need more forms you can download them for free at our website. Your field notes should include today's date and your location (the name of the wetland you are exploring if it has a name). Write about today's weather: the temperature, what the sky looks like, and so forth. You can also use this form to list the plants and animals you see or to just write about the way you are feeling when you explore wetlands. You can write before, during, or after your walk.

Read the Signs of Nature

When you take a wetlands walk you are a naturalist. A naturalist is someone who studies nature. A naturalist looks for tracks and scat—signs that animals are nearby. He smells the air for fragrant flowers or stinky animals. He listens for birds, insects, and other animals. He uses his eyes, ears, and nose to help him find signs of nature.

This duck is drawn by Naseehaa Bacchus, age 9, of Clarksburg, MD.

Need more room to draw or write? Use blank paper or download free forms at www.takeawalk.com.

Go! Boogie in a Bog

Bogs are unique wetlands. They are a special place to see one of the most unusual **adaptations** in nature—meat eating plants! These are plants that eat insects because they can't get nutrients from the soil in a bog. They eat insects because the soil contains a high amount of acid and acid prevents soil nutrients from reaching the plants.

The acid also prevents bacteria from growing and, as a result, when something dies in a bog it takes a very long time to decompose. Partially decayed vegetation is called *peat*. (Once the body of a man, dead for 2,000 years, was found in a bog in Denmark, nearly perfectly preserved. They should have called him "Pete". ☺)

When you explore a bog look for meat-eating plants like Pitcher Plants. Watch for mammals, such as deer, bears, bobcats, hares, and beavers, that visit the bog looking for food. Look for insects and listen for birds. Which plants and animals you see depends upon the location of your bog.

Pitcher Plants (top) are carnivores. Because they eat insects, they are also called insectivores. Sphagnum moss (middle) grows on the surface of peat in a bog. It is sometimes called "peat moss". Did you know that we grow cranberries in bogs? When the berries are ready to be picked we flood the bog and they float to the surface where we can gather them by machine (bottom).

New Words?

Adaptation
(a-dap-TAY-shen)
Changes that a species makes to help it survive when its environment, food sources, or world changes. Adaptations take place over many generations.

What's for Dinner?

Look inside pitcher plants and you might find a trapped insect on the menu.

Where in the U.S.?

Bogs are found mostly in the New England states, the Great Lakes states and across eastern Canada.

Bogs aren't the only peaty wetland. Another is the *fen*. A fen is different from a bog in that the soil is highly alkaline (low in acid) and a fen is fed by groundwater. Fens have lots of peat but, because of their nutrient-rich soil, they also have lots (and lots) of wildflowers. If you want to see wildflowers and butterflies visit a fen.

This American Bittern was drawn by Emma Giordano, age 11, of Moorestown, NJ.

Living Proof

I'm not kidding when I say that you can see a lot of species of birds in an estuary. On one of the days I was researching for this book, Rob and I took a walk at The Wetlands Institute in Stone Harbour NJ. During our short walk we saw: Laughing Gulls, Willets, Red-winged Blackbirds, and Osprey (the Institute has a webcam on one of the nests). We saw flocks of Double-crested Cormorants flying overhead. We also saw both Great and Snowy Egrets, a Little Blue Egret, and both Greater and Lesser Yellowlegs. We heard Eastern Bluebirds and Clapper Rails. We saw Barn Swallows, Boat-tailed Grackles, Short-billed Dowitchers, Black Oystercatchers, Brants, and Mallards. We didn't keep a list so we can't remember all of the birds. Maybe some day you'll be as good at identifying birds as we are.

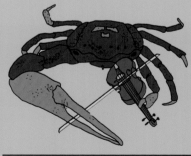

Clap your hands and stamp your feet,
If a Fiddler Crab you meet.
With one large claw and one that's little,
He doesn't really have a fiddle.
But if you close your eyes, they say
You'll hear his happy music play!

Estuaries are ocean bays or river mouths where freshwater from a river mixes with saltwater from the ocean. This mixed water is called *brackish* water. Estuaries are very important wetlands—they produce more organic matter per acre each year than farmland. Within estuaries are several kinds of habitats including rocky shores, mud flats and salt marshes. And if you want to explore a cool wetland, you definitely should experience a salt marsh.

The thing about salt marshes is that you don't have to actually go into them—you can "explore" a salt marsh with a decent pair of binoculars or a spotting scope. You can view salt marshes from the roadside or from a building; on a deck or through a window.

You can explore by boat, too. Have you ever taken a salt marsh tour boat? They're so much fun and very educational. You can also explore like I do, from a kayak. If you like coastal wetlands you might like my book, "Take a Beach Walk".

I took this photo of a salt marsh at sunset in New Jersey. I call it "birds in the cordgrass". The tallest white bird is a Great Egret and the shorter white birds are Snowy Egrets. They were having dinner. The gray, black and white birds in the background are the Black-crowned Night Herons. Can you guess why I think the night herons were having their breakfast?

The Northern Harrier is a hawk that hunts over the grasses of the marsh. He is easily recognized by the white patch just above his tail.

14

You can find a lot of species of birds in salt marshes. See if you can identify the wetlands specialists: the ones with adaptations like long beaks to probe the sand and mud for food, long legs to wade or stand in the shallow water to catch food, or webbed feet to help them move through the water and walk on mud.

There's a lot of cordgrass in a salt marsh, too. Seriously, a lot! Cordgrass belongs to a group of plants adapted for salty conditions called *halophytes* (HAL-oh-fites). Some grass grows under the water. Eelgrass is an example. Eelgrass is important because it serves as a critical nursery and shelter for shrimp, minnows, scallops, eels, mussels, crabs, clams, horseshoe crabs, and juvenile fish.

When you explore a salt marsh, look up, down, and all around! During one walk, Rob and I came across a Diamondback Terrapin. It is the only species of turtle in North America that spends its life in brackish water. The turtle had just hatched and was on its way to the water when it crossed our path. Luckily Rob was carefully observing during our walk or we might have stepped on the turtle. Thanks, Rob! You're the best!

Rob helped this Diamondback Terrapin cross the path. He held it long enough so I could get this photo of the plastron. Look at the tiny size of this terrapin in Rob's hand! I was so excited I forgot to ask Rob to turn the turtle over so I could photograph the carapace.

Eelgrass grows under water (above) and is important and delicate. It needs our care and protection.

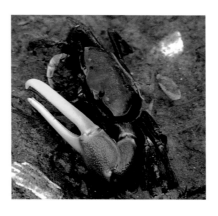

A Fiddler Crab gets its name from the male's giant claw.

Phil's Smorgasbord

Phil Broder, the Director of Education at The Wetlands Institute in Stone Harbor, NJ, sees the salt marsh as a cafeteria. He writes:

Fish. Shrimp. Crabs. Clams. Mussels. Lobster. Oysters. Scallops. Fishsticks. If you eat seafood, you have to love wetlands. About two-thirds of the commercially-caught seafood in America spends some part of its life in a salt marsh. Looking across the marsh at acre after acre of cordgrass, you might think, "Whoopie, big deal". Grass isn't all that exciting, right? But that grass provides the nutrients that make the marsh work and let everything else grow big. So whether you're dropping a line in the water on weekends or hauling nets on a commercial fishing boat, you need to realize that wetlands put food on our tables and money in our pockets. No wetlands, no seafood. It's that simple.

To learn more about The Wetlands Institute, visit: **www.wetlandsinstitute.org**

Who Cares? They Do!

Save The Bay is the oldest and largest organization working exclusively to protect, restore and celebrate the San Francisco Bay. Learn more at: **www.savethebay.org**

Go Meet the Magnificent Music...

Wetland Plants

Another adaptation of wetland plants is how they grow in wet areas. Some grow under the water, some float on it, and others come up through the water. Wetland plants can be divided into three groups that describe how they grow: emergent, submergent, and floater.

Emergent plants grow in water but part of the plant sticks up above the water. A good example of this is the Common Cattail.

Submergents grow completely under the water (submerged). Most are rooted in the ground. An example of this kind of plant is eelgrass (page 15).

Floaters are plants that are rooted but float on the surface of the water, such as lilies. Some floaters are free-floating, like Duckweed.

Keywords and Phrases

To learn more search for "freshwater marshes" on the Web.

Frog by Francesca Aimone, age 9, of Manahawkin, NJ.

Sometimes you can hear a marsh long before you see it, thanks to a few species of birds and a little frog. The Canada Geese, Mallards, and Red-winged Blackbirds form a marsh chorus that sings the arrival of spring.

Marshes are also recognizable by their plants with soft stems like cattails, which grow in the shallow water and provide habitat for animals. You can hear birds flitting around in the cattails and, if you stand still long enough, you might see them too.

Parts of the cattail are edible. Native Americans used the cattail plants for medicine.

The Red-winged Blackbirds are my favorite birds of the marsh. I love their "konk-ar-REEEE" call. Every spring I look forward to their return. The males usually return to the marshes before the females to claim their territory. They defend their territory and when strangers are near (like me) they give an alarm call. My friend Jim Peck explained to me that dominant males get the best territories. They are the ones with the biggest, brightest red patches on their shoulders. Now I identify the dominant males in a flock. See if you can.

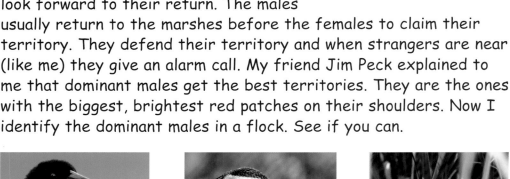

Males (above, left) and females (above, center) of the Red-winged Blackbird look very different. They weave nests in the reeds and males defend their territory.

...Makers of Freshwater Marshes

Spring Peepers are tiny frogs that make one heck of a large noise. They're found in the eastern half of the U.S. and Canada. They're *nocturnal* —active at night. During the night the marsh is alive with their calls that sound like a thousand tiny bells jingling. Every spring I look forward to hearing the Spring Peepers and I sleep with the windows open just to hear them.

Canada Geese graze, nest, and honk in marshes, lakes, bays, and rivers. If there is open water they will spend the night in the water where they are safe from predators. You can often see and hear large groups of geese coming into the water near sunset in the spring, fall, and winter.

Mallards quack me up! Ask a friend to make a duck sound and they would say "quack". That's the call of the female Mallard. Males make soft sounds. Like Canada Geese, these ducks can make any spot—even your backyard—their habitat and nesting site, but they are partial to marshes.

When you are in a marsh look near the cattails and reeds for animals. Listen for frogs, birds and owls. Look near flowers and in sunny mud puddles for butterflies. Scan the shallow water for wading birds, fish, and dragonflies. Watch for waterfowl flying overhead. Look on the ground for animal tracks. Marshes can be loud, exciting places or, at other times, quiet and peaceful.

The Spring Peeper frog is very small—they average about one inch. They're hard to see but easy to hear.

During nesting season, adult Canada Geese molt—grow new feathers. Therefore, they don't fly. They stay on the ground or in the water with their youngsters.

Feathers on the male Mallard's head are iridescent. Sometimes they look blue, other times green.

Prairie Potholes

Prairie potholes are a special kind of wetland that appear on the Great Plains in Iowa, Nebraska, Minnesota, North and South Dakota, Montana, and the western provinces of Canada. These small ponds and marshes were formed about 10,000 years ago! But they have been disappearing since the 1800's when settlers began draining them to farm the land. The prairie potholes are an important habitat for many species, especially migrating waterfowl.

Who Cares? They Do!

Conservation organizations are working to preserve and protect prairie potholes. One is called **Ducks Unlimited**. Learn more at: **www.ducks.org**

A Ring-necked Duck doesn't wear a diamond ring around its neck. It is named for a purplish ring around it's neck that is hardly visible.

Isabella's Insect

My friend Isabella Weigert of Lincoln, Nebraska, is very interested in an endangered insect called the Salt Creek Tiger Beetle. She wrote this information about the beetle so I could share it with you:

The Salt Creek tiger beetle, a bioindicator of the environment found only in a few Nebraska saline wetlands, is named for capturing prey in a "tiger-like" manner. It is one of the most endangered insects in America because of habitat loss.

It has a 4-stage life cycle. Egg, larva, pupa and adult. Males sit on females after mating to discourage suitors.

In 2002, 777 beetles were found. In 2005, 153 beetles were found. Then the U.S. Fish and Wildlife Service put it on the Endangered Species List. A survey done in 2007 found 263.

Can we afford to lose an entire ecosystem?

Isabella also painted the beautiful Wood Duck below.

Wood Duck by Isabella Weigart, age 10, of Lincoln, NE.

Streams make me want to take off my shoes, put my feet in the water and become part of the perfect picture. The sound of water trickling over rocks and roots is a magnet to me. During the writing of this book, I frequently asked people where they would prefer to spend an hour—by a river, stream, lake or pond—and why. Almost everyone said "stream" and "the sound of the water".

But rumor has it that at least one mammal doesn't like the sound of running water. Beavers are master builders that live in rivers, streams, lakes, ponds, or marshes. They eat poplar, willow, aspen, birch, and maple trees. They also build dams and lodges (homes) from trees. They use their tails to warn other beavers of danger by slapping them on the surface of the water. Some people say that the Beaver builds a dam to muffle the sounds of the rushing water. I don't know if that's true but I do know Beavers can slap hard with that tail!

Beavers (top) live in most of the U.S. and Canada. They use their tail as a rudder when they swim. The tail also stores fat for the winter. This beaver painting (bottom) was done by Morgan Sloan, age 12, of Moorestown, NJ.

One day, while kayaking on my lake, I saw a Beaver. I tried to get close enough to take a picture. But when I got close, it slapped the water with its tail and got my camera wet. Oh well, that's one picture that wasn't meant to be.

...Relax By a River

No matter where you live in North America, chances are you are not far from a river or stream. On a hot summer day, a shaded river or stream is a great place to cool off. Summer is also the best time to explore rivers and streams. There are lots of plants and wildlife just waiting for you to discover—and finding them is easy. Rivers and streams are great places to see trees, wildflowers, turtles, salamanders, snakes, river otters, insects, and birds. One of my favorite riverside birds is the Eastern Phoebe whose name comes from its call, "fee-BEEEE".

What should you look for and where should you look when you take your river or stream walk? Look in the water for fish, snakes, and insects. Look at the pattern of sand or rocks on the bottom that gets created by the moving water. Look *on the banks* for basking turtles. The banks are the edges of the land along the water. Look under rocks (but put them back) for salamanders and beetle larvae. Scan the trees for nesting birds. Keep an eye out for butterflies on the wildflowers and dragonflies laying their eggs in still pools of water. Be careful when you walk on rocks because algae (that slimy green stuff) can make them very slippery. Don't forget to take a minute to enjoy the sounds of the moving water.

The American Dipper (top) is a western bird that can stand in shallow, rushing water, which makes it look like it is water skiing! This Eastern Phoebe (middle) has caught a dragonfly for dinner. This is the Small Mayfly (bottom). Mayfly adults live just one day—long enough to breed and lay eggs.

Rivers and Streams

What's the difference between rivers and streams? Streams are filled by rain and snow (precipitation) or underground springs. They flow into rivers. Rivers are filled by streams and precipitation and they flow into seas.

Where I live we call streams "creeks" and some people pronounce that word "crick". But no matter what you call them: rivers, rivulets, creeks, or streams, there's no doubt we are all attracted to the sound of moving water. Animals are attracted to the sound, too. Rivers and streams are a major source of water and a great place to see wildlife.

Keywords and Phrases

To learn about another streamside bird search for "waterthrush" on the Web.

Wetlands by Dane Dimuzio, age 7, of Houston, TX.

Hear the Loon's call:

Search for "Common Loon" on the web and you'll find plenty of websites where you can play a recording of the loon's call. Warning: it's craaaaazy! ☺

Wetlands Careers

There are lots of careers that focus on wetlands. Here are a few that might interest you:

Wetland Scientists
Specialists who study wetlands—and wetland plants, soil, water, animals or the entire ecosystem.

Wetland Caretakers
People or groups dedicated to preserving, caring for, or educating others about wetlands. For an example, search "riverkeepers" on the Web.

Wetland Regulators
People or groups that enforce wetland laws and regulations, and oversee the use of wetlands.

Common Yellowthroat by Taylor Johns, age 11, of Moorestown, NJ.

Lakes are places where we go boating, skiing, fishing, swimming, and walking. They are habitats of plants and animals. They are where we get our drinking water. Lakes can be big or small, man-made or natural. The difference between lakes and ponds is that lakes are generally deeper than ponds. As a result, water temperatures can vary in the different depths of lake water—especially in the summer. Lakes are important breeding grounds to many species of waterfowl (swimming birds, such as ducks and geese).

Lakes and ponds are good places to observe waterfowl. Also look for animal tracks near the water, dragonflies laying eggs on the water, insects like Water Striders walking on the water, and mammals bathing in or drinking the water. Look in sunny spots on rocks and logs for snakes and turtles. Watch for fish in the water. Look for water lilies in the water and wildflowers on the banks.

Common Loons nest in northern lakes with forests. The expression "crazy as a loon" comes from this bird's call which you have to hear to believe!

Duckweed is a tiny plant that can practically cover the surface of the quiet water in lakes and ponds. Duckweed is a favorite food of ducks—I guess that's how it got its name.

A Pondhawk is not a bird. It is a dragonfly. There are Eastern and Western species. Males are green and females are blue. You can see them around lakes and, you guessed it, ponds!

...Visit a Vernal Pond

There's a special kind of pond that is, perhaps, the most exciting wetland. It is a *vernal pond*. And survival there is a race against time. *Vernal* means spring. A vernal pond (also called a vernal *pool*) is a spring wetland. The pond is filled by melting snow or rain. By summer, most vernal ponds dry up.

Vernal ponds are a happening places if you want to see tadpoles and salamanders. But both tadpole and salamander larvae have to metamorphosize into adults that can breathe air and crawl on the ground before the pond dries up or they will dry up with it! You won't find Bullfrog tadpoles in a vernal pond because they can take up to 3 years to become adults. Fish are predators of young salamanders and frogs. But fish can't survive in a vernal pond, either. Therefore, vernal ponds make great nurseries.

Snakes, turtles, drag-onflies, damselflies, and other insects call vernal ponds their spring homes.

Look for vernal ponds after heavy rains in March. Happy Hunting!

Adult salamanders (like this Spotted Salamander, top) emerge from hibernation in spring and make their way to vernal ponds to lay eggs. This one was photographed by Roberta Dell'Anno, mom of Teresa and Peter (see sidebar). Wood Frogs (middle) depend on vernal ponds for their survival—they lay their eggs only in vernal ponds. They are very small—This one is dwarfed by blades of grass. Tiny creatures called Fairy Shrimp (bottom) lay their eggs in vernal ponds. The eggs can remain dormant for months and even years, ensuring survival of the species even during dry times.

Family Ponding

My friends Peter and Teresa Dell'Anno live in Andover, MA. They wrote this about ponding:

Every year in late March after a heavy rain, my mom says, "Let's go vernal pooling." We walk into our garage and my mom grabs a couple of pairs of full-body fishing waders. They are heavy and look pretty strange. I mean, really! Imagine seeing someone walking down the street at night in giant, bulky, rubber overalls!

We arrive at a small pond and step into the murky waters with our flashlights and nets in-hand to look for fairy shrimp, wood frogs, spring peepers and yellow-spotted salamanders. Most of the salamanders we find have yellow spots. But on rare occasions, we find one with blue spots!

We must be careful where we step or we may go right under and it's hard to get up if our waders fill with water! I know from experience. Ponding is fun to do with family or friends. Enjoy! —Peter, age 12

All the things that happen at the ponds are messy, dark, slimy and absolutely fun! We walk in dark water at night with all sorts of things scattering about all over the place. Everyone plunges into the water for frogs and salamanders. I caught at least three frogs! I saw a lot of yellow-spotted salamanders but they were too fast for me. My mom had to catch those. We also got a slimy newt and cool water bugs! —Teresa, age 9.

Go! Swoosh in a Swamp

Wetland Threats

What do you think are the major threats to our wetlands? Here are a few:

Agriculture. We drain wetlands to grow food. Chemicals from our farms seep into our water. Farm animals graze wetlands and leave no food or shelter for wildlife.

Development. Will we ever stop taking nature's habitat and redesigning it for our own? We build on wetlands and our buildings and roads block normal drainage.

Land-based sewer systems. Sewage treatments plants drain into wetlands.

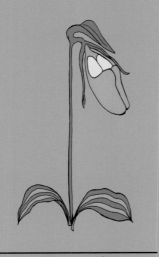

There is a slipper you can't wear
Not in the house; not anywhere
You should not lift it off the floor
You cannot find it in a store
It doesn't fit a single foot
It doesn't move it must stay put
You cannot wear it or collect it
This pretty slipper is protected
It can be found in swamps and bogs
And it eats meat but never frogs
It can close but has no zipper
It's the Showy Lady's Slipper

A swamp has more woody plants and fewer soft-stemmed plants than a marsh. Swamps are soggy, wet places and, depending on their location, home to a huge woodpecker, a stinky plant named after a mammal, and an orchid named after a woman's shoe.

The Pileated (PY-lee-ata-id or PILL-e-ate-id) Woodpecker is as large as a crow (about 19"). Keep your eyes and ears open for this huge, flashy woodpecker. For a very long time it was thought to be the largest living woodpecker in North America. But the Ivory-billed Woodpecker, slightly larger, similar looking, and thought to be extinct, has been reported recently in Arkansas.

An early sign of spring in the swamp is Skunk Cabbage. Skunk Cabbage is neither a skunk nor a cabbage, but is a plant that starts growing so early in the spring it often comes up through the snow. Although it has an odd name, if you step on it you'll understand why it is called Skunk Cabbage. Another odd name for a plant, in this case a wildflower, is the Showy Lady's Slipper. I do think it's showy, but a slipper?

Swamps are a great place to see trees, wildflowers, birds, ferns, amphibians, reptiles, and insects.

The Pileated Woodpecker (top) is the biggest woodpecker I've ever seen! Skunk Cabbage (middle) is a good reason to watch where you're walking in the swamp. The Showy Lady's Slipper (bottom) is the state flower of Minnesota.

Go! Explore the Everglades

The Florida Everglades is one of the most famous wetlands in the world. It is a huge watershed with as many as nine distinct habitats that include marine, estuary, and freshwater wetlands. Thanks to some popular theme parks, lots of families vacation in Florida. I hope, if yours does, you'll include a side trip to the Everglades to experience this unique wetland.

Most people know that there are American Alligators in the Everglades. But did you know that there are American Crocodiles there too? You can also see the Anhinga—a bird that dives to catch its food. Its nickname is "snake bird" because when it swims only its long neck and head stick out of the water and it looks like a snake. Anhingas can dive because they lack the oils in their feathers that keep other birds, like ducks, afloat.

One endangered and special resident of the Everglades is the Snail Kite. Not a snail, not a kite, but a hawk, the Snail Kite eats—guess what—snails!

The Everglades are home to some species of plants and animals that can be found nowhere else in the world! I hope you get to visit the Everglades some day.

American Alligators (top) can live as long as fifty years. The Anhinga (middle) must occasionally leave the water to dry its feathers in the sun. The favorite food of the Snail Kite (right) is the Apple Snail. This male is keeping his from the female.

More Wetland Threats

Oil spills. Every time we have an oil spill from a ship carrying oil, animals get covered with oil and they usually die as a result. As long as we continue to need and use as much oil as we do in this country, we'll continue to have to live with oil spills.

Litter and Storm drain run-off. Although rainwater is pretty clean when it falls from the sky, a heavy rain can cause flooding, which can then wash every bit of trash that was lying around into the rivers and the ocean.

Non-native Plants. Non-native plants have no natural predators in wetlands and therefore take over. Native plants that play an important role in the wetlands are choked out by non-natives.

More Types of Swamps

Forested swamps have deciduous trees. **Shrub** swamps have more shrubs than trees. **Mangrove** swamps are coastal wetlands with brackish water where the trees, shrubs and other plants are salt-tolerant.

Wetlands by Austin Aultman, age 8, of Seminary, MS.

Go! Remember Your Walk With a...

George on Notes

My friend, George Ambrose, loves to explore wetlands and take field notes. Follow his advice and you'll take good field notes that will help you identify the plants and animals you see:

Record the time, date, and weather to help with identification because certain species prefer certain weather or time of day.

Write good descriptions. For example, "a tall plant with narrow green leaves and a dark brown thing on top that looks like a hotdog on a stick" might be one way of describing a cattail.

Draw a plant or animal and label the colors of the body parts on your drawing if you don't have color drawing instruments in the field.

Read more of George's advice in the sidebar of the next page.

Here's an example of how to create a Nature ID Page. The facing page is a blank form for you to write down details about a plant or animal you see on your wetlands walk. You can draw it or take a photo of it and paste it on your form page. If it's a species you don't recognize, your notes will help you to identify the species when you research it in a field guide, at the library, or on the Web.

Date: August 29, last days of summer vacation.
Time: 11 AM
Weather Conditions: 80 degrees, sunny with some clouds.

Habitat and location: Marsh Creek State Park

Size and physical description: Really big bird! Maybe three feet tall! Long neck and long legs. Gray, white and black all over. Long feathers on the back of its head.

Behavior Observation (if it is an animal): Standing very still in the water and sticking its head in to catch and eat fish and frogs..

Additional Notes: This bird ate a fish that was so big I could see the shape of the fish in his neck!

Species Name:
Great Blue Heron.

Great Blue Heron by Megan Donovan, age 10, of Boyds, MD.

...Nature ID Page of Your Own

Date:

Time:

Weather Conditions:

Habitat and location:

Size and physical description:

Behavior Observation (if it is an animal):

Additional Notes:

Species Name:

(Optional) Make a drawing or paste a photo here:

George on Lists

George also says you should make lists of what you see. You can use your Field Notes on page 12 if you like. George suggests that you list the birds, frogs, snakes, flowers, and other plants you see. A variety of species (called biodiversity) is one indication of how healthy a wetland is. The more species you see, the healthier the wetland.

Thanks for your great advice, George Ambrose!

Celebrate Wetlands

February 2 is World Wetlands Day. Learn more at **www.ramsar.org**

May is American Wetlands Month. Learn more at: **www.iwla.org**

Bite-size Bits

Frogs have very small teeth along their upper jaw. Salamanders have small teeth on their upper and lower jaws. Turtles have no teeth—which explains to me why they look like my Uncle Harry!

Need more room to draw or write? Use blank paper or download free forms at www.takeawalk.com.

Go! Identify Birds

The birds on these two pages are a sampling of the most common birds of wetlands with the most widespread ranges in North America. They are not in any particular order. The key (below) indicates the wetlands they inhabit. See other birds on the following pages:

American Dipper	19	Great Egret	14
Anhinga	23	Mallard	17, 20, 32
Bald Eagle	3	Northern Harrier	14
Black Crowned Night Heron	14	Pileated Woodpecker	22
Canada Goose	17	Red-winged Blackbird	16
Common Loon	20	Snowy Egret	back cover, 14
Eastern Phoebe	19	Snail Kite	23

B Bogs
E Estuaries
G Everglades
L Lakes & Ponds
M Marshes
P Prairie Potholes
R Rivers & Streams
S Swamps

Bufflehead
B,L

Pied-billed Grebe
L,M

Eared Grebe
L

Green-winged Teal
L

Wood Duck
S

Northern Shoveler
M,P

American Widgeon
E,M

Gadwall
M

Blue-winged Teal
E,L,M

Northern Pintail
E,M

Common Goldeneye
L

Ruddy Duck
M

Go! Identify Birds

Canada Goose
L,M,R

Mute Swan
L,R

Great Egret
E,M

Great Blue Heron
E,M,L,R

Black-crowned Night Heron
E,M,R,S

American Bittern
E,M

Green Heron
E,L,M,R

American Coot
E,L,M

Spotted Sandpiper
E,L,M

Osprey
E,L,R

Short-eared Owl
M

Belted Kingfisher
L,R

Marsh Wren
E,M

Yellow-headed Blackbird
M

Common Yellowthroat
E,M,R

Did You Know?

Laws protect our wetlands. The Clean Water Act (CWA) of 1972 was established to protect our waterways and stop pollution from being discharged into U.S. waters.

Go! Identify Plants

The plants and animals on these pages are a sampling of the most common plants and animals of wetlands with the most widespread ranges in North America. They are not in any particular order. The key (below) indicates the wetlands they inhabit.

B Bogs
E Estuaries
G Everglades
L Lakes & Ponds
M Marshes
P Prairie Potholes
R Rivers & Streams
S Swamps

Golden Ragwort
S

Yellow Pond Lily
L, R

American Lotus
L, R

Blue Flag
M, S

Cotton Grass
B

Duckweed
L, R

Arrowhead
E, M

Purple Loosestrife
M

Venus Flytrap
M

Swamp Rose Mallow
M

Turk's Cap Lily
M, S

Jewelweed (Touch Me Not)
S

Go! Identify Reptiles and Amphibians

Stinkpot Turtle
L, R

Wood Turtle
S

Spiny Softshell Turtle
L, R

Western Pond Turtle
L, M

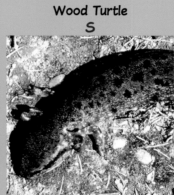

Spotted Salamander
S

Mudpuppy
L, R

California Newt
L, R

Eastern Newt
L

Southern Two-lined Salamander
R

Tiger Salamander
L, R

Four-toed Salamander
B

Northern Cricket Frog
L, R

Northern Leopard Frog
L, M

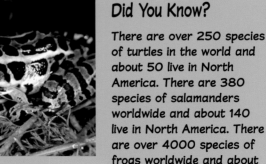

Pickerel Frog
R, S

Did You Know?

There are over 250 species of turtles in the world and about 50 live in North America. There are 380 species of salamanders worldwide and about 140 live in North America. There are over 4000 species of frogs worldwide and about 88 in the U.S. and Canada.

Go! Identify Mammals

The plants and animals on these pages are a sampling of the most common plants and animals of wetlands with the most widespread ranges in North America. They are not in any particular order. The key (below) indicates the wetlands they inhabit.

See also:

B   Bogs
E   Estuaries
G   Everglades
L   Lakes & Ponds
M   Marshes
P   Prairie Potholes
R   Rivers & Streams
S   Swamps

River Otter
E, L, R

Mink
E, M

White-tailed Deer
B, E, S

Raccoon
E, S

Muskrat
M

Black Bear
B, E, S

Bobcat
E, S

Moose
L, S